Stegosaurus

and other Jurassic Plant-Eaters

by Daniel Cohen

Capstone Press

MINNEAPOLIS

Capstone Press • 2440 Fernbrook Lane • Minneapolis, MN 55447

Editorial Director   John Coughlan
Managing Editor   Tom Streissguth
Production Editor   James Stapleton
Book Design   Timothy Halldin

Library of Congress Cataloging-in-Publication Data
Cohen, Daniel, 1936-
    Stegosaurus and other Jurassic plant-eaters / Daniel Cohen
      p. cm. -- (Dinosaurs of North America)
    Includes bibliographical references (p. 41) and index.
    Summary: Describes what is known about four different
  kinds of dinosaurs that lived in parts of the United States
  millions of years ago.
    ISBN 1-56065-287-X
    1. Stegosaurus--Juvenile literature. 2. Apatosaurus--
  Juvenile literature. 3. Brachiosaurus--Juvenile literature.
  4. Diplodocus--Juvenile literature. [1. Stegosaurus.
  2. Apatosaurus. 3. Brachiosaurus. 4. Diplodocus.
  5. Dinosaurs.] I. Title. II. Series: Cohen, Daniel, 1936--
  Dinosaurs of North America.
    QE862.O65C626   1996
    567.9'7--dc20   95-11234
                                            CIP
                                            AC

Table of Contents

Chapter 1

When They Lived

Millions of years ago, long before humans appeared, **dinosaurs** ruled the earth. It was an age of giants. The largest land creatures that have ever lived fought to survive in a world much different from our own. It was the **Jurassic** (joo-RASS-ic) period.

The Jurassic period lasted from about 195 million to 140 million years ago. Modern human beings have been on earth for only about 40,000 years. That gives you an idea of

just how long the Jurassic period lasted and how long ago it was.

Dinosaurs first appeared on the earth about 210 million years ago, during a period of geological time called the **Triassic** (try-ASS-ic) period. The earliest dinosaurs were fairly small and not very numerous. It was not until the Jurassic period that dinosaurs really became rulers of the land.

The Jurassic World

At one time all the land masses in the world were clumped together in a single supercontinent. By the Jurassic period, the supercontinent had slowly begun to break up and drift apart. But the world's land masses

Small mammals first appeared during the Jurassic period, an age when dinosaurs were a dominant species on the planet.

Quaternary Age
1.8m to present

65m	Tertiary Age	1.8m
140m	Cretaceous Age	65m
195m	Jurassic Age	140m
230m	Triassic Age	195m
280m	Permian Age	230m
345m	Carboniferous	280m
395m	Devonian Age	345m
435m	Silurian Age	395m
500m	Ordovcian Age	435m
700m	Cambrian Age	500m

Birds
Mammals

Reptiles
Amphibians

Fish
Primitive chordates

were still a lot closer together than they are today.

The climate was very different as well. There were no polar ice caps and the range of temperatures worldwide was not nearly as great as it is now. The weather patterns were more regular and there were fewer severe storms. Most Jurassic dinosaurs could probably have lived on land anywhere in the world.

Jurassic Life

Dinosaurs were not the only creatures in the Jurassic world. They shared the land with small mammals, which resembled modern shrews and mice. Dinosaurs and our ancestors, the mammals, appeared on earth at about the same time. But for millions of years the dinosaurs were much more successful.

Jurassic plants were different from the plants we are familiar with today. There were no modern types of trees and no flowering plants. But ferns and cycads, which are primitive plants, grew nearly everywhere in the warm and swampy landscape. Some of these

plants grew to enormous sizes and provided food for the large number of Jurassic **herbivorous**, or plant-eating, dinosaurs.

The Jurassic period lasted about 55 million years. During those millions of years the earth changed. The continents drifted farther apart. The climate became less regular and uniform.

And during those millions of years, the dinosaurs themselves changed. Dinosaurs that had flourished at the start of the Jurassic became extinct by the end of the period. Many new **species** of dinosaurs first appeared during the Jurassic. By the end of the period, dinosaurs were far more successful and dominant than they had been at the beginning.

Stegosaurus

STEG-oh-SAW-rus
roofed reptile
Length: *25 feet (7.5 meters)*
Weight: *2 tons (1.8 metric tons)*
Range: *Western United States*

The Stegosaurus is one of the most familiar and one of the strangest of all

dinosaurs. It is best known for the double row of flat plates that extended from just behind the head, down the back, and halfway along the tail.

Puzzling Plates

Scientists have long puzzled about the plates. Most believe that they stood straight up in a double row, like a spiky fence. Some think the plates lay flat on the creature's back to form a protective shield. The plates may have protected the creatures from attacks by large meat-eating (**carnivorous**) dinosaurs.

But plates have never been found actually attached to the skeleton of a stegosaurus. So no one really knows how they were arranged.

It is also possible that the plates were not armor at all but were covered by a thin layer of skin rich in blood vessels. Built like this, they could have served as a simple system for heating and cooling. Turned toward the sun, the blood vessels would absorb heat when the animal was cold. They could be turned away

from the sun to lose heat when the animal became too hot.

No one really knows what the plates were for, but they did give the huge dinosaur its name. In Greek, stegosaurus means roofed reptile, after the plates that formed a roof over its back.

Dangerous Spikes

There can be no doubt about the purpose of the spikes at the end of the creature's tail. They would have been a highly effective weapon. A solid blow from the spiked tail would have discouraged even the largest and hungriest predators.

Another striking feature of the Stegosaurus is its tiny head. A full-grown Stegosaurus weighed more than 2 tons (1.8 metric tons), yet its brain was only about the size of a walnut. That is a small brain even for a dinosaur.

Stegosaurus remains were first identified in the 1870s, quite early in the history of dinosaur discoveries. There have also been several

Stegosaurus had a brain about the size of a walnut.

excellent specimens found. This has made Stegosaurus one of the best known of all the dinosaurs. The tiny brain of this famous creature helped to contribute to the idea that all dinosaurs were slow moving and extremely stupid.

Stegosaurus had a large bundle of nerve tissue at the base of its tail. At one time, this

led to the belief that Stegosaurus had two brains. But this large area of nerve tissue was not a second brain. It was probably the area where all of the nerves of the back legs and tail came together. It might have formed a large relay station for messages and signals on their way to and from the brain.

A Successful Dinosaur

Stegosaurus was a slow-moving creature. It lumbered along, eating ferns and other plants that grew close to the ground. It depended on

A Stegosaurus model stalks the Denver Museum of Natural History.

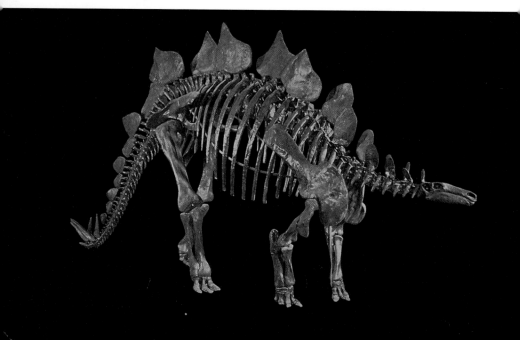

its armor, strong spiked tail, and large size to protect itself from enemies.

Recent research indicates that even the small-brained Stegosaurus was not as slow moving and stupid as was once believed. They did not drag their tails and they probably lived and traveled in large herds–another form of protection from predators.

Small-brained or not, Stegosaurus was an extremely successful dinosaur. **Fossil** remains of it and several closely related species are abundant, especially in the American West. Many skeletons have been found in Colorado, Utah, and Wyoming.

Stegosaurus first appeared in the middle of the Jurassic period and continued to flourish right to the end of the period, when it and all closely related species became extinct.

Apatosaurus was called Brontosaurus for many years. Its name was officially changed in 1979.

Apatosaurus

a-PAT-oh-SAW-rus
deceptive lizard
Range: *Western United States*
Length: *70 feet (21 meters)*
Weight: *36 tons (32.4 metric tons)*

T he more familiar name of this famous
dinosaur is Brontosaurus (bron-TO-SAW-rus),

or thunder lizard. There is a great deal of confusion in dinosaur names. The Apatosaurus controversy is by far the most famous of these naming controversies.

Robert Owen's Name

Here is how it came about. The person who discovers a new dinosaur, or any new species of plant or animal, is given the honor of naming it. In 1841, British scientist Sir Robert Owen first used the word dinosaur, which comes from the Greek words for terrible lizard or terrible reptile. Dinosaurs are certainly not lizards. They may not even be reptiles. But the word saurus, meaning lizard or reptile, is now attached to every dinosaur name.

In the 1870s there was a whole series of remarkable dinosaur discoveries in the American West. Among the most spectacular was the discovery of the fossil remains of a gigantic creature with a small head, long neck, huge thick body, and long tail. It was the biggest dinosaur ever found, and it soon became the most famous.

Unfortunately, fossils are rarely complete. Scientists may only be able to recover a small portion of the bones of any single individual. The bones of different individuals and sometimes different species are often mixed together. It is easy for scientists to make mistakes. It was even easier back in the 1870s when paleontologists, who study past life on earth, were just beginning to learn about dinosaurs.

Apatosaurus or Brontosaurus?

Making the problem of identification even more difficult in the 1870s was an angry rivalry between two of the leading scientists and fossil collectors, Othniel Charles Marsh and Edward Drinker Cope. Both men were working in the newly discovered fossil beds in the West. They were making remarkable discoveries every year. But each man wanted to claim credit for every discovery, and each rushed to name the creatures that they found. In their haste, they were sometimes careless.

Marsh was the one who first found fossils of the creature. He called it Apatosaurus. His rival Cope, however, found what appeared to be an even better specimen. He was the first one to build a reconstruction of the creature, which he called Brontosaurus. It was his name and his picture of the dinosaur that were accepted and became so famous.

Unfortunately for Cope, there are many different kinds of gigantic, long-necked

dinosaurs that lived in what is now the American West during the Jurassic period. The bones of several different species were mixed up together in his find. The reconstruction he made was not accurate.

For a long time many scientists suspected that something was wrong with Cope's identification. But it was not until 1979, nearly a century after the name Brontosaurus had first been accepted, that the name was officially changed back to Apatosaurus.

Since Brontosaurus was one of the best known of all dinosaur names for so many years, the change has created confusion. Even the U.S. Postal Service made a mistake. A few years ago, when it introduced dinosaur stamps, one of the stamps showed a gigantic long-necked creature called a Brontosaurus.

Brachiosaurus would have weighed more than a dozen elephants.

Brachiosaurus

(BRAKE-ee-oh-SAW-rus)
arm lizard
Range: *Western United States*
Length: *80 feet (24 meters)*
Weight: *66 tons (59.4 metric tons)*

Brachiosaurus is one of the large and highly successful group of Jurassic dinosaurs

known as **sauropods**, or lizard-footed dinosaurs. They all have small heads, long necks, thick bodies, and massive, tapering tails.

The Brachiosaurus looks different from other sauropods because its front legs are much longer than its back legs. It was this unusual feature that led discoverers to give it a name that meant arm lizard. When the sauropod dinosaurs were first discovered, many scientists thought that they were simply too massive to be able to move efficiently on land. The scientists speculated that the giants spent much of their time in the water, and that the water supported their bulky bodies.

Strange Nostrils

Brachiosaurus had nostrils on the top of its head. It was once believed that this allowed the creature to breathe while its body was entirely under water.

This view of Brachiosaurus changed in the 1970s, when scientists reexamined the evidence and decided the creature could not

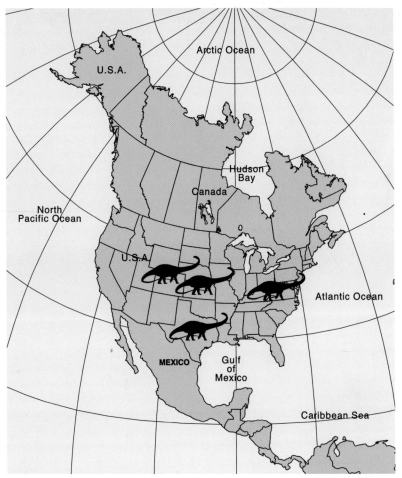

The remains of Brachiosaurus have been found in the United States as well as in Africa and Europe.

have lived in the water. It would not have been able to breathe, because the pressure of the water would have collapsed its lungs.

Scientists are now convinced that Brachiosaurus lived on land and ate the tops of tall trees. The enormous neck would have given it a long reach. The whole body sloped down from the highest point at the shoulders, like a modern giraffe. Such a body would have allowed its neck an even greater reach.

A Brachiosaurus could easily have looked over the top of a four-story building. It would have weighed as much as a dozen elephants, which are the largest land-living creatures today.

The Ultrasaurus

Brachiosaurus is the largest dinosaur for which a complete skeleton has been discovered. But fragmentary remains of what appear to be similar, but even larger, dinosaurs have been found in Colorado. The largest of these has been called Ultrasaurus. More complete remains must be found before Ultrasaurus can be officially recognized as a separate species.

What these bones indicate is that Ultrasaurus was nearly one-third larger than Brachiosaurus. It could have looked over the top of a five-story building. This would make it by far the largest known land animal ever. Partial remains of a similar, but somewhat smaller, dinosaur called Supersaurus have also been found in the same Colorado area.

Are Ultrasaurus and Supersaurus the largest dinosaurs that ever existed? Are they the last word in dinosaur size? No one really knows.

Not so very long ago, many scientists thought Brachiosaurus was too massive to be able to support itself out of the water. Now they know its size did not keep it from being an active and very successful land animal. The world of dinosaurs still holds many surprises.

Diplodocus

(dip-LOD-oh-kus)
double-beam reptile
Range: *Western United States*
Length: *90 feet (27 meters)*
Weight: *12 tons (10.8 metric tons)*

Diplodocus is the longest of the known dinosaurs. It was built along the same basic

27

lines as Brachiosaurus, Apatosaurus, and the other sauropod dinosaurs. It had a small head, long neck, thick body, and tapering tail. But Diplodocus was more elongated and more lightly built than the others. While it was much

Diplodocus ranged over what is now the Great Plains and the Rocky Mountains.

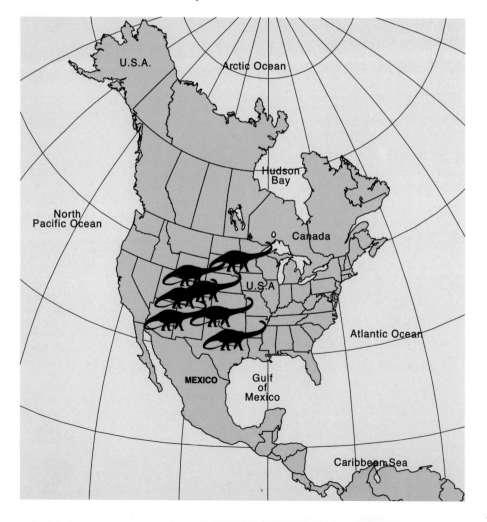

longer than Apatosaurus, it weighed a mere 12 tons (10.8 metric tons)–only one-third as much.

A Practical Tail

The most notable feature of this dinosaur was its long whiplike tail. The tail was nearly as long as the body and neck combined. It was probably Diplodocus's habit to rear up on its hind legs and bend its tail around to form a sort of third leg for balance. Stretching up with its long neck, it would have been able to browse on the uppermost cones and leaves of the **coniferous**, or cone-bearing, trees that grew in abundance in the Jurassic landscape.

The largest of Jurassic predators, like Allosaurus, might have been able to attack Diplodocus. But, while the creature lacked armor or spikes, it would not have been an easy target. The long flexible tail, powered by great back muscles, could have swept clear a large area around the animal. The tail's whiplash end could have stunned or even killed a predator. Diplodocus would also have been able to rear

up on its back legs and bring its big front legs crashing down on an attacker.

A full grown and healthy Diplodocus would probably have been safe from harm. Individuals that were not yet full grown, or those who were sick or injured, would have been easier targets for the big meat-eaters.

A Herd of Diplodocus

Like all the sauropods, Diplodocus had a very tiny brain. At one time, scientists assumed that the creatures were stupid and slow moving. Scientists now believe that while the sauropods probably were not very smart, they were intelligent enough to live and travel in large herds. In a herd, the adults could have more easily protected their young from predators.

A herd of sauropod giants rumbling over the Jurassic landscape would have been one of the most impressive sights in the long history of life on earth. It would have taken an enormous amount of vegetation to feed one of these

creatures. A herd of them would have stripped an area bare in a short time.

The Diplodocus Diet

Scientists are still unsure of how the giants were able to find enough to eat. It is difficult to imagine how these creatures, with their tiny heads and relatively small and weak teeth were able to grab and swallow enough plant life in a day to keep themselves alive. They must have had to eat almost constantly. And when they were not eating they were looking for food.

Whatever problems Diplodocus and the other sauropods might have had, they were able to overcome them. These dinosaurs were extremely successful and numerous throughout much of the Jurassic period.

Extinction

By the end of the Jurassic period, however, their numbers had declined dramatically. Only a few of the smaller sauropods survived into

the next period, the **Cretaceous** period. The **extinction** of Diplodocus and similar species is probably the result of changes in climate or vegetation or both. But no one is really sure. All we do know is that by the start of Cretaceous period, about 140 million years ago, the largest of the dinosaurs had already disappeared.

Chapter 3

How Dinosaurs are Discovered

We know that dinosaurs roamed the earth millions of years ago. Yet their remains continue to be discovered by scientists even now. How is it possible that dinosaur bones can be preserved for so many years? The answer lies in the process of fossilization.

When a dinosaur died, several different things could happen to its body. Animals may have eaten its flesh. Smaller animals and even bacteria could have eaten and removed the soft tissue of the dinosaur. Many times, the

dinosaur bones could have been crushed or broken as the flesh was removed from the skeleton. So it is possible that many dinosaur bones simply disintegrated before they could be preserved by nature.

Turning into Rock

However, many dinosaur remains in desert climates were covered with windblown sand before they could be eaten or decompose. Others were washed into lakes or rivers and

A paleontologist carefully digs for remains of a dinosaur skeleton.

covered with mud. As the years went by, more and more sand and mud covered these dinosaurs. Over time, this sand and mud turned into rock. Over the course of thousands of years, chemicals in the rocks seeped into the dinosaur remains and turned them into rock, too. The hardened dinosaur remains are then called fossils.

Footprints made by dinosaurs have also been preserved by becoming fossils. So have dinosaur eggs, nests, and dung. All dinosaur fossils provide scientists with valuable information about these incredible animals and their life on earth.

Buried in Rock

Dinosaur fossils have been found on every continent on earth. In most cases, they are buried in rock. Scientists attempt to unearth the fossils carefully with as little damage as possible to the remains.

The first step in excavating, or removing the fossils from the earth, is to take away the

surrounding soil and rock. Large diggers and bulldozers do this work until the fossils are close to the surface. Then scientists work with small hand tools like hammers and chisels to remove the remaining rock.

Careful Record-Keeping

Once the fossils are exposed, the scientists take great care to record everything they find. Bones are measured and photographed. Extensive notes and diagrams record exactly how the skeleton parts are connected.

As the bones are removed from the digging site, they are numbered and recorded. Then they are carefully packed into padded crates. If a bone is weak or crumbly, it is not removed until it is sprayed with a special hard-setting foam. Sometimes, plaster-soaked bandages are used to harden the bone.

Once all the fossils have been recorded from a site, they are carefully shipped to the scientists' laboratories. There the bones are rebuilt to show how the dinosaur looked while it was living and the dinosaurs ruled the earth.

Glossary

carnivorous–a meat eater

coniferous–a cone-bearing plant

Cretaceous–the third geological period in the Age of Dinosaurs from 140 million to 65 million years ago

dinosaur–a special group of animals that dominated life on earth for 150 million years

extinction–the death of a group of plants or animals

fossil–the preserved trace of an ancient plant or animal

herbivorous–a plant eater

Jurassic–the second geological period in the Age of Dinosaurs from 195 million to 140 million years ago

paleontology–the scientific study of life in past ages

sauropod–an order of gigantic dinosaurs with small heads, long necks, heavy bodies, and long tails

species–a group of animals that look the same and can breed together

Triassic–the first geological period in the Age of Dinosaurs from 230 million to 195 million years ago

To Learn More

Arnold, Caroline. *Dinosaur Mountain: Graveyard of the Past*. New York: Clarion Books, 1989.

Benton, Michael. *The Dinosaur Encyclopedia*. New York: Julian Messner, 1984.

Carroll, Susan. *How Big is a Brachiosaurus? Fascinating Facts About Dinosaurs*. New York: Platt & Munk, 1986.

Cohen, Daniel and Cohen, Susan. *Where to Find Dinosaurs Today*. New York: Cobblehill, 1992.

Lasky, Kathryn. *Dinosaur Dig*. New York: Morrow Junior Books, 1990.

Lauber, Patricia. *Dinosaurs Walked Here and Other Stories Fossils Tell*. New York: Bradbury Press, 1987.

___. *Living with Dinosaurs*. New York: Bradbury Press, 1991.

Lindsay, William. *The Great Dinosaur Atlas*. New York: Julian Messner, 1991.

Murphy, Jim. *The Last Dinosaur.* New York: Scholastic, 1988.

Sandell, Elizabeth. *Apatosaurus: The Deceptive Dinosaur.* Mankato, Minn.: Bancroft-Sage Publications, 1989.

Stefoff, Rebecca. *Extinction.* New York: Chelsea House Publishers, 1992.

Wallace, Joseph E. *The Audubon Society Pocket Guide to the Dinosaurs.* New York: Knopf, 1992.

Wilson, Ron. *Diplodocus*. Vero Beach, Fla: Rourke Enterprises, 1984.

Some Useful Addresses

The Academy of Natural Sciences
19th Street and The Parkway
Philadelphia, PA 19103

The American Museum of Natural History
Central Park West at 79th Street
New York, NY 10024-5192

California Academy of Sciences
Golden Gate Park
San Francisco, CA 94118-4599

Dinosaur National Monument
P.O. Box 210
Dinosaur, CO 81610

Field Museum of Natural History
Roosevelt Road at Lake Shore Drive
Chicago, IL 60605-2496

Museum of the Rockies
South Sixth Street and Kagy Boulevard
Bozeman, MT 59717-0040

National Museum of Natural History
Smithsonian Institution
Tenth Street and Constitution Avenue N.W.
Washington, DC 20002

**Natural History Museum of Los Angeles
  County**
900 Exposition Boulevard
Los Angeles, CA 90007

New Mexico Museum of Natural History
1801 Mountain Road
Albuquerque, NM 87104

The Peabody Museum
170 Whitney Avenue
New Haven, CT 06511

Royal Ontario Museum
100 Queen's Park
Toronto, Ontario M5S 2C6
Canada

Tyrell Museum of Paleontology
Box 7500
Drumheller, Alberta T0J 0Y0
Canada

Where to View Dinosaur Tracks

Dinosaur Ridge

This is a national landmark near Morrison, west of Denver, Colorado. The hiking trail allows visitors to stroll along a trackbed from the Cretaceous period.

Dinosaur Valley State Park

This park is in Glen Rose, southwest of Fort Worth, Texas. Part of an original dinosaur trackway was excavated here. It is on view at the American Museum of Natural History in New York City.

Dinosaur State Park

Visitors to this park, in Rocky Hill, south of Hartford, Connecticut, can make plaster casts of dinosaur tracks.

For more information on dinosaur events and sites, write to:

Dinosaur Society
200 Carleton Avenue
East Islip, NY 11730
(516) 277-7855

This organization promotes research and education in the study of dinosaurs. It also publishes *Dino Times*, a monthly magazine for children. Subscriptions are $19.95 a year. *Dinosaur Report*, a quarterly magazine, costs $25 a year.

Photo credits: Royal Tyrell Museum of Paleontology: p. 4; James P. Rowan: pp. 13, 19, 23; Denver Museum of Natural History: pp. 14, 30-31.

Index